FREE TO IMAGINE

Refocus Outreach Services

ADULT  EDITION

MATERIALS NEEDED FOR THE DREAM JOURNEY

DREAM BOARD MATERIALS:
ONE MINI TO LARGE POSTER BOARD
YOUR CHOICE OF MARKERS/COLORED PENCILS/CRAYONS
CLEAR TAPE
GLUE STICKS OR LIQUID GLUE
MAGAZINES (FOR INSPIRATIONAL WORDS AND IMAGES)
A LIST OF INSPIRING WORDS OR QUOTES (STICKERS CAN BE USED)

REMEMBER: Dream goals can be created with PowerPoint, Google Docs, other online document creation options, or with traditional scrapbooks and photo albums. Choose which option best fits your creativity and lifestyle.

NOW, LET'S DREAM!

DREAMING IS FREE

WELCOME to the Free to Imagine Dream Board workshop!

Refocus Outreach Services invites you to join us on the journey of discovering your next LIFE step. What we mean by your next LIFE step is finding out what energizes you, what brings excitement and fulfillment to your life. We are here to help you identify your gifts, talents and see your dreams come to pass. Team Refocus is dedicated to empowering you with the tools needed to accomplish the dreams you decide to pursue. Our desire is to see your dreams made possible through encouragement, creativity, and hard work as we partner with you.

Think about these questions:
- What other goals do I want to pursue?
- What else do I have to offer to others?
- What am I good at doing?

Yours truly,

Coach David & Coach Nita
Team Refocus

Table of Contents

Session 1	Your Dream Journey	6
Session 2	Keep Moving Forward and Build	10
Session 3 -	Dream Challenges	14
Session 4 -	Positive Mindset	18
Session 5 -	Keeping Your Dreams/Goals Alive	23
Completion Certificate		26
Calendar Pages		27
Journal Pages		30
About the Authors		33

YOUR DREAM JOURNEY

SESSION 1

Purpose of this session:
We want you to think about what excites you. Take time to remember or create a dream you always wanted to do. Think outside of the box. Dig deep and dream big.

"It always seems impossible until it's done." ~*Nelson Mandela*

Put Into Action:
Think about a dream or idea you had that came to fruition. Think about the details of that dream/idea. Where were you when you thought about it? Did you share it with anyone? How did it make you feel? What did you see? *(excerpt from Dream Journey, 2012)*

Write down a dream/idea you accomplished and how it made you feel:

Who did you share your dream/idea with?

How long did it take to accomplish?

ACTIVITY

MAKE A DREAM LIST

Write down 30 dreams/goals you want to accomplish this year. This process will take thought and time. Be creative. No need to rush. Take the limits off and dream bigger. Start your list in class and then take time outside of class to add to it. Ask yourself the following questions as you create your list:

- If money were not an issue, what would you do?
- If you had the time and resources, what would you want to do?
- If you knew you could not fail, what goal would you want to accomplish?

	Date Dreamed	Date Achieved
1.		
2.		
3.		
4.		
5.		
6.		
7.		
8.		
9.		
10.		

ACTION

MY DREAM LIST   Date Dreamed   Date Achieved

11. _____
12. _____
13. _____
14. _____
15. _____
16. _____
17. _____
18. _____
19. _____
20. _____
21. _____
22. _____
23. _____
24. _____
25. _____
26. _____
27. _____
28. _____
29. _____
30. _____

Never Stop Dreaming

THESE ARE YOUR DREAMS!

WHAT DO YOU DESIRE?

BE CREATIVE!

WHO ARE YOU BECOMING?

Don't Dream Your Life
Live Your Dream

GO AFTER YOUR DREAM!

SESSION 2 - KEEP MOVING FORWARD & BUILD

"Passion is energy. Feel the power that comes from focusing on what excites you."
Oprah Winfrey

Purpose of this session:
You thought about your dreams and wrote down ones you found to be important. Now, it is time to choose. Pick a goal/dream you want to work on.

Before you choose, think about the one goal you are most passionate about?

You become what you think about yourself! What has your focus? Think about your dreams daily as you tend to move toward the things you are thinking about. Take small steps toward your dreams every day.

Put Into Action:
Ok, now write it down. This will be the one you will work toward in this class.

Dream/Goal: _____

_____

S.M.A.R.T. GOAL

SPECIFIC - Set a clearly-defined goal.
Do you know clearly what goal you want to accomplish?

MEASURABLE - Keep count of your progress along the way.
How will you know that you have reached your goal?

ATTAINABLE- Set goals you are passionate to reach without others.
Does meeting this goal solely depend on someone else's input?"

RELEVANT- Determine what goals are important enough to pursue. What would you like to work on?

TIME-BASED - Deadlines are important in order to really reach a goal.
What's your best guess for when this will be done?

Narrow down what your S.M.A.R.T. goal will be (meaning break it down):

_____

Choose a partner to share your goal. Give each other feedback. Re-create the S.M.A.R.T goal if necessary.

ACTIVITY

FOCUS FORWARD

Time to move forward with your S.M.A.R.T. goal by taking action steps. "What will you do? When will you do it?"

Write down some action steps: Think outside the box.
Take the limits off.
Think big!

_____

_____

_____

_____

_____

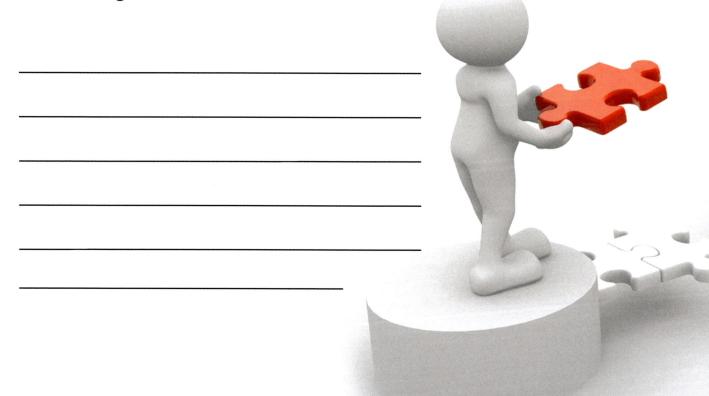

ACTIVITY

"Don't mistake movement with progress!" -Denzel Washington

Make your steps matter. Keep moving forward, no matter the obstacles. Every step does make a difference.

Dig Deeper: To help you determine some additional action steps, think about what you can accomplish that does not depend on others?

ADDITIONAL ACTION STEPS:

_____

_____

_____

YOUR DREAM JOURNEY

SESSION 3 - DREAM CHALLENGE

PURPOSE: We want to prepare you for the hard times; the times you may feel like you want to quit. There are going to be times when nothing seems to be working even when you put your best foot forward. What will you do with your dreams when it gets tough?

CHALLENGE = To dispute the truth or validity of something.

OBSTACLES = A thing that blocks one's way or prevents or hinders progress.

At times, while moving forward in pursuit of our dreams, there may be obstacles we have to overcome. For instance, over the last year you saved $8,000 for a dream vacation. You worked hard, made sacrifices, refrained from hanging out with family and friends, and saved money by preparing meals at home and shopping less.

Now, within the month, you will go on a trip to Jamaica with a few friends. Unfortunately, an emergency comes up that wipes out half of your savings. Do you give up on the trip?

WHAT DO YOU DESIRE TO DO?

Some situations in life may seem like lemons. You can either stay in the sour state of disappointment OR decide to be creative and make lemonade out of those challenges. How bad do you want to accomplish the goals set before you?

The choice is up to you.

TIME TO PICK

Action – Review your dream list. Pick a dream and think of some possible challenges or obstacles you could be faced with on the way to accomplishing that dream?

Write it down.

_____

_____

_____

_____

_____

ACTIVITY

BE SOLUTION-MINDED

Keep in mind, that with each obstacle you are faced with there are solutions to overcome those challenges. These solutions can come from your own creativity or from the input of others. It is essential to have someone— or several people in your life you can count on to help you to endure life challenges.

Now take time to write down solutions to overcome the challenges from the above dream activation exercise.

Write them down:

_____

_____

_____

_____

ACTIVITY

GROUP ACTIVITY

Pick a partner and discuss your dream and the challenges you could possibly face. Then, talk about the solutions you came up with. After each person has a turn, ask your partner for a solution to help you overcome possible obstacles. Write down solutions. What resources you may have access to? If you are doing this exercise alone take time to reflect and write solutions to overcome a challenge or challenges.

Dig Deeper: Answer the question below and be prepared to discuss your action steps to overcome discouragement.

Accountability is key to accomplish your goals. Know that disappointment may come as you move forward to fulfill your dreams. What will you do when discouraged by those challenges? What might keep you from getting where you want to go?

YOUR DREAM JOURNEY

SESSION 4 - POSITIVE MINDSET

PURPOSE: We encourage you to focus and be mindful of what you think about. If you have a mind to win, you will. The opposite is true as well. When you think you will fail you may fall short. We choose what to focus on! Do you have any internal thoughts or beliefs about yourself that may hinder you from accomplishing your dreams?

Put Into Action - Flush it!
When faced with self doubt we may become our own worst critic. What we chose to think about ourselves is key to move forward with our goals or quit while in the middle of progress. As we talked about in our previous session, obstacles are inevitable. Since we all know it is possible to be discouraged, we must prepare for the battle of our minds.

George was finishing his last semester of undergrad. He was maintaining a high B average in most classes and could see himself walking across the stage in less than three months to accept his bachelor's degree in business administration. He was so excited that he had his mother send out the invitations to his graduation party. Everybody was expected to be there. Yet, that excitement was short lived. One class that still gave him trouble—economics. George could not sleep or eat due to the fear of failure. He hired a tutor, family and friends attempted to help him study, but nothing seemed to ease his nervousness. So, George stopped going to class and turning in assignments for almost three weeks.

Write down what you think and feel about the scenario:

_____

_____

If you were faced with a similar situation, what things would you do differently to ensure you graduate on time?

If George were your friend, what advice would you give him?

What you believe about yourself will determine the outcome of your goals. If you have allowed self-doubt to govern you, today let us make a step in the right direction and change the way we think. It is time to adopt a healthier and more positive mindset.

Flush the old mindset!
Welcome the new way of thinking!

ACTIVITY

TAKE OFF THE LIMITS!

What you believe about yourself will determine the outcome of your goals. If you have allowed self-doubt to govern you, let us take a step in the right direction and change the way you think.

Think and write down your new way of thinking when faced with self-doubt:

_____

_____

_____

_____

_____

_____

REFLECTION

HAVE A GO-GETTER MINDSET

Are you one who goes after what you want, or do you wait for others to present opportunities to you? To move forward with your dreams, you have to be the pilot, not copilot, who drives you toward your dream goals. Any additional help you receive is just *extra* help. Be thankful for the help, but you are responsible for your own destiny.

What are your next steps to achieve your goals? Are your priorities in order? Be productive in your journey. Busyness does *not* equal productivity.

As you move along, make sure to reaccess that your steps are really working toward the goal. Go after your most important goal. An attempt to accomplish multiple goals at one time can become overwhelming and may cause you to quit.

ACTIVITY

Dig Deeper:
Come prepared to discuss at next session: What are some things you can do to prepare yourself for the next opportunity in you fulfilling your dream/goal?

_____

_____

_____

_____

_____

_____

YOUR DREAM JOURNEY

SESSION 5 - KEEPING YOUR GOALS ALIVE

PURPOSE: We want you to put your dreams where you will see them every day. We want you to be the driving force behind seeing your goals come to pass. Are you passionate about your dreams? How important is this dream to you? If you are the only one keeping your dream from going forward, will you continue to pursue this dream? Are you willing to pay the price for your dream?

Put Into Action- Creating the Dream Board
Let us tie all we have learned into creating this year's Dream Board.

What will be the most important dream you decide to pursue? Do not bombard yourself with too many goals at one time. Focus on the one goal in front of you. Once you complete it, then move to the next one.

Stay Future Focused

Team Refocus – Coach David and Coach Nita

innovation

change • vision • strategy • idea • creativity • inspiration

GET CREATIVE!
GET BRAVE! • GET EXCITED!

The Dream Board Workshop Certificate of Completion

_____

Name of Participant:

_____

Location / Program Name:

_____

Date of Completion:

Coach David   Coach Nita

YOUR DREAM JOURNEY

YOU DID IT!

Team Refocus wants to thank you for your participation in this *Free to Imagine Dream Board* workshop. We encourage you to continue moving forward to accomplish your goals.

- Revisit your dreams and keep them alive by looking at them daily.
- Place your dream board where it can be seen.
- Speak out loud what you hope to achieve.
- Share your goals with others who support your vision.
- Keep track of completed goals, cross them off your Session 1 list.
- Celebrate when you complete a goal.
- See yourself fulfilling the goals you wrote.
- Create a new board every year…and keep going after your dreams!
- Use the enclosed blank calendar and journal pages to keep track of your goals.

Coach David and Coach Nita

Refocus Outreach Services: Mark the days you worked on your goal(s).

MONTH						YEAR
SUNDAY	MONDAY	TUESDAY	WEDNESDAY	THURSDAY	FRIDAY	SATURDAY

Keeping track of your goals will keep you accountable and encouraged.
Take the time to put an "x" or a "check mark" on the dates you worked or completed your goal.

Refocus Outreach Services: Mark the days you worked on your goal(s).

MONTH				YEAR		
SUNDAY	MONDAY	TUESDAY	WEDNESDAY	THURSDAY	FRIDAY	SATURDAY

Keeping track of your goals will keep you accountable and encouraged.
Take the time to put an "x" or a "check mark" on the dates you worked or completed your goal.

Refocus Outreach Services: Mark the days you worked on your goal(s).

MONTH						YEAR
SUNDAY	MONDAY	TUESDAY	WEDNESDAY	THURSDAY	FRIDAY	SATURDAY

Keeping track of your goals will keep you accountable and encouraged.
Take the time to put an "x" or a "check mark" on the dates you worked or completed your goal.

Journal Pages

Date: _____

Journal Pages

Date:

Journal Pages

Date:

Journal Pages

Date:

Journal Pages

Date:

Journal Pages

Date: _____

Journal Pages

Date:

Journal Pages

Date:

Journal Pages

Date:

Journal Pages

Date: _____

Journal Pages

Date:

Journal Pages

Date:

Journal Pages

Date:

Journal Pages

Date:

ABOUT THE AUTHORS

As cofounders of REFOCUS OUTREACH SERVICES David Jones and Janita Lane are passionate about helping clients recognize and overcome life obstacles, make healthier choices, and set realistic and attainable goals. The team specializes in helping achievers of all ages push past the limitations of life and create new possibilities through interactive and inspiring Refocus Dream Board workshops.

David Jones, a.k.a, Coach David, is a motivational speaker and a certified life coach. He strives to share his passion for life while celebrating others who accomplish their goals. Coach David continuously spends time in the public school sector in Kalamazoo, Michigan where he teaches the importance of literacy. As a father, he also promotes the value of learning and literacy in the home. He founded the *Fathers Do Read* program as an effort to see fathers and their children build a healthier and long-standing positive relationship through the exploration of books. As a certified life coach and mentor, Coach David shares his life experiences with youth and adults in hopes of helping them successfully create positive ways to overcome daily life challenges.

Janita Lane, a.k.a., Coach Nita, has seen firsthand how life struggles can hinder a child's desire to reach their fullest potential. As a mother of two young adults she is a certified life coach who strives to help others see their potential. She believes anyone can achieve any goal when they have a plan, patience, and persistence. Coach Nita encourages clients—both young and old, to see the greatness they possess when they accomplish their dreams. She earned bachelor's degree in Family Life Education to help equip individuals and families with the knowledge and skills to enhance their well being.

The coaches have inspired youth through their Dream Board workshops not to let their current environment limit their potential at such places as the Kalamazoo (Michigan) County Juvenile Detention Center, Michigan Youth Charter Academy, and Lakeside Children Academy. In addition to youth, they have worked with the seniors of Heritage Community of Kalamazoo to encourage them to continue to set goals toward an even more fulfilled life. Refocus Outreach Services has also worked in Kalamazoo schools, summer camps, and women's conferences.

Free to Imagine: Dream Board Workbook

Copyright 2020 Refocus Outreach Services

All rights reserved. This workbook or any portion thereof may not be reproduced or transmitted in any form by any means without written permission from Refocus Outreach Services, Inc.

For more information on bulk orders, book sponsorships, speaking engagements or workshops, please send correspondence to:
Refocusoutreachservices@gmail.com

Published by Refocus Outreach Services
in collaboration with Fortitude Graphic Design & Printing and Season Press, LLC

By Janita Lane and David Jones
Edited by Sonya Hollins, Season Press, LLC
Designed by Sean Hollins, Fortitude Graphic Design & Printing

Summary: What happens when you dream big? *Free to Imagine: Dream Board Workbook* will provide the tools needed to unlock your dreams, display them, and watch them come true!

Adult Edition ISBN: 978-1-7353600-2-7
Student Edition ISBN: 978-1-7353600-1-0

FIRST EDITION
10 9 8 7 6 5 4 3 2 1

Printed in the U.S.A.

References:

Coaching Questions: A Coach's Guide to Powerful Asking Skills by Tony Stolzfus, 2008, www.coach22.com Dream Journey Workbook by Andy & Janine Mason, 2012. The Dream Checklist by Jack Canfield.

Made in the USA
Monee, IL
18 October 2020

Refocus Outreach Services

$12.95
ISBN 978-1-7353600-2-7

Ann Marie, the Noisiest Kid in the Class

A Tell and Show™ Book

story by Lindy Brown

illustrations by